The Journey Deep Within

Julian Elijah Deabanico

Presentation by *BookLeaf Publishing*

Web: www.bookleafpub.com

E-mail: info@bookleafpub.com

ISBN: 9789395969574

First edition 2022

DEDICATION

To God, my family and friends for always being there.

ACKNOWLEDGEMENT

Glory be to the Father, to the Son and to the Holy Spirit. As it was in the beginning, is now and will be forever.

PREFACE

Maybe one day these words will find you-

I tried.

I really did.

Distant

Tell me dear,

How to live,

Afar from you,

Bereft of your presence,

When everything I do,

Leads me back to you.

And just when I'm sure,

I already got over you,

There you were, standing.

In my dreams last night.

Right Time

Then as I sat alone,

All I ever think,

Was what could've been,

In silence, words not said.

As it all fell to pieces.

Now, I hear the wind's hum,

See all shades and hues,

Feel my pulse and breath.

Finally, know this is the time,

To fully give myself,

But you already left.

Deep regrets and buried wishes.

I should've prepared years ago.

Bear With Me

I am never still,

    On an eternal chase-

    Hopping on one and another.

    Oh! For one to escape

    What I would give,

    This prison I'm in,

    Crafted by my mind.

If my heart indeed reigned

    Myself would I ever forgive?

    When all it ever says,

    Please, I want you to stay.

Desolate Goodbye

Unpredictable as the days,

And the ebb and flow of waves,

Your presence come and go,

Lest I come as you say so.

But, each time you disappear,

my heart's longing dear.

Truly don't know if I can keep,

Myself from this forlorn trip.

At times, I look up at the serene sky,

As my heart lets out a sigh,

Whispers on my ear I adored,

Turned to crumbles, I abhor.

Imagined chains latched on you,

Every single bit fractured me,

Clicks and clacks awakened me,

Now I'm starting, letting you free.

Relations and Strings

I looked at the people around me,

And felt I have so much to lose

When these faces are all gone,

Permanently plastered in time's history.

I've never felt my heart so full,

As on garish days like this,

When the world's love is on me,

And mine as directed to them.

To give one's heart and time to others,

And to receive warmth and affection,

Without conditions and deceit,

Is the kind of life I aspire to live.

When all seems barren and dismal,

Turn to the faces you adore,

And in their loving company

Relish and find propensity

For all the good things in life.

As I Am Here and Now

I ain't worth much,

But what your eyes see,

Is all I can ever give.

Despite this bleakness,

And my heart's meager offer,

One hopes you care for it,

As I am, is wholly yours.

Under a blanket of stars,

I'm wondering how you are.

If only you were here,

I'd be my happiest.

But you're not

And Im constantly,

Wondering about you,

And how you've been,

Late night long talks-

Became short and sharp

Even as seldom,

As a passing star,

Is it me or is it fate

That's not meant to be,

Two shining stars.

In determinate points.

But alas, as long as the night's dark,

And the shadow's cast are abound,

I'll cast my ephemeral light,

For you to always find me.

For you know I am,

Always here and now.

Illusion

Each day I miss a glimpse of you,

I wonder if you are even true,

As days pass without your voice,

I'm filling what was once your void.

Me thinks it's for the best,

But my heart refutes to lay rest,

Nonetheless, when all is said and done,

Maybe time gives due to what is mine.

Let's Try

After everything that transpired,

You're still the one I aspire.

Much willing to try your pace,

Understanding behind that face.

Will this ever work?

I have doubts.

With purest intentions,

I leave no remark.

Solitude

As I sat alone with solitude,

Many things come to mind.

What am I living for?

Who I truly am?

Where is life going?

Why am I here?

How can I escape from it all?

There was silence, but my self.

The answer reverberated louder,

The darkness enveloped everywhere,

Short fitful sobs afar became mine.

Answers that are clattered amidst the chaos.

I'm going nowhere, until it dawned on me

I am sitting still with solitude, fighting for peace.

Gratitude

There is light within,

    It has been from the start.

    My self and rambles shrouded it.

    But it never left my side.

To hear His words speak to me,

    Oh! What great delight,

    How I wish His words be mine.

    His good life, as my own be my sacrifice.

Right Here

Caress you tighter, I'll do,

If it eases all the pain,

To make you forget,

The worries and fears,

Churning in your head.

Ill stay and wait more,

Until tears turn bland,

Bear your load, but not easy,

If it means side by side we walk.

I may have a chance, I may not.

As nights pass, it knows I tried.

Heartstrings

I was cutting strings,

    Still not done, I know,

    For I can still feel things,

    Too deeply if asked of me.

Wish it can be snapped once.

    so remembrance is miles from me,

    Prolly when all comes to end,

    The strings and me lays side,

    For Strings still became a part of me.

Rest

Finally my weary heart and soul,

Can now face the day's lot,

Without your life's details.

Not even wanting to know,

How close the breeze is to your skin,

How your eyes laid on the sky,

And how you laughed with him.

I got too close and it's my undoing.

It took time, and some more days.

But at last, with a hopeful heart,

Someday, I'll find my needed rest.

Self-love

Too harsh on myself,

I dreamt of being a lot,

Tried to run away,

To see myself just the same.

Now, the inside voices settled.

But, my shadows haunt still.

Probing for light til none,

I just stood where I stand.

Looking at my beating heart.

Lies a speck of light as dust,

Breathe. I still have love to give,

This time it's for mine to keep.

Lessons Learned

Crippled by much waiting,

For those two letters,

You could've easily given,

That would make my day.

Now I'm just here waiting,

For life to tell my story,

Im starting to walk again,

Facing the road head high.

No soul taught me about pain,

Stifled sobs til I pass out,

and wake a bit tad complete.

I did and faced it all,

Lost count for I started small.

Cloudy Days

There are wakeful days,

I can conquer everything,

Even then, clouds shroud over me,

I just let it pass away,

For all of those are days of me.

Action is my personal antidote,

Discipline both my friend and foe,

To eventually stand up and do,

One's etched responsibilities,

Despite my mind's and soul's,

Feeble attempt and countless wish,

For a restful eternal slumber.

Know Not How to Love

I've made you too perfect in mind,

My shining beacon of hope,

Smile as divine as starlight,

A mind of centuries old wisdom,

Caring hands that nurture life,

and a beauty that grips my sanity.

When the glass fell, my trust broke,

Rose-colored lenses washed by disdain,

It will never be the same again.

So much pain, but with tear-cleared eyes,

I'm seeing it all as it truly is.

I've made you too perfect in my mind.

But, it was I who knows not how to love.

The War Inside

I'm putting down my sword,

To end all the countless wars,

Ensuing deep within my skin,

Causing all this self-inflicted misery.

I'm raising the white flag up,

Not to signify accepting defeat,

Nor leaving you to go drown.

It's a high road for our peace,

I hope you follow through this pact,

That my blood and wounds bring,

So we can finally be at peace,

To call my self, myself and my friend.

From The Start

Nothing is as constant and true,

As my friend and ultimate foe.

On days it propels me forward,

And on some, tethered to bed.

Visions ten years from now,

Pushed at the brink of mind,

Imaginary fantasies of night,

Turn to morn's harsh realities.

When all I could ever want,

Was within a fingertips reach,

She never moved, so pain came closer.

Nothing is as constant and true,

As my friend and ultimate foe-

Pain has been here since I think,

Til now - be and bear my load, it is.

Curiosity

I wake up to yet another day.

My ruthless mind thinks, again?

I see and live each day in monotony,

Already disheartened to start the day.

I feel like it's already too familiar,

But my mind thinks to react-

This moment's breathe differs than past,

The sun did shine, but not where it was,

I cried, but for a different reason;

The wind still passed, on a new season.

Don't be that fool, living life bleakly.

There's something new, if you look closely.

Hope

This is the death of me,

Or that's what I believed

When the deafening silence,

Took over my mind and peace.

But with each passing moment,

Leads me to a reality,

One I didn't know exist,

Where I am one, connected to all.

It was a singular feeling,

I kept on pushing far,

Suppressed within myself,

With parts I'm unaware.

Then past the threshold,

    Of uneasiness in my core,

    Burns a blinding light,

    And a keen sense of freedom.

I say amidst all the pain,

    I can bear this after all,

    The silence that killed me.

    Brought me a new life.

www.ingramcontent.com/pod-product-compliance
Lightning Source LLC
LaVergne TN
LVHW021344200726